Backyard Bug Mazes

by Roger Moreau

Sterling Publishing Co., Inc.
New York

This book has been inspired by Brian

10 9 8 7 6 5 4 3 2 1

Published by Sterling Publishing Co., Inc.
387 Park Avenue South, New York, NY 10016
© 2006 by Roger Moreau
Distributed in Canada by Sterling Publishing
^{c}/o Canadian Manda Group, 165 Dufferin Street
Toronto, Ontario, Canada M6K 3H6
Distributed in the United Kingdom by GMC Distribution Services,
Castle Place, 166 High Street, Lewes, East Sussex, England BN7 1XU
Distributed in Australia by Capricorn Link (Australia) Pty. Ltd.
P.O. Box 704, Windsor, NSW 2756, Australia

Printed in China

Sterling ISBN-13: 978-1-4027-2846-4
ISBN-10: 1-4027-2846-8

Contents

Suggested Use of This Book   4

Introduction   5

Background Information   6

The Bug Manual   7

The Sizing Machine   8

The Scrap Wood Pile   9

Termites   10

Earwigs   12

Cockroaches   14

Tarantula   16

Centipedes   18

Monarch Butterfly   20

June Bugs   22

Praying Mantis   24

Dragonflies   26

The Backyard   28

Black Widow Spider   30

Ant Hole   32

Ant Colony   34

Attack of the Ants   36

Aphids   38

Grasshoppers   40

Tomato Worms   42

More Tomato Worms   43

Snails and Slugs   44

Corn Worms   46

Honey Bee   47

Hive   48

The End of the Day   50

Back Into the Sizing Machine   51

Congratulations!   52

Answers   53

Index/Books by the Author   80

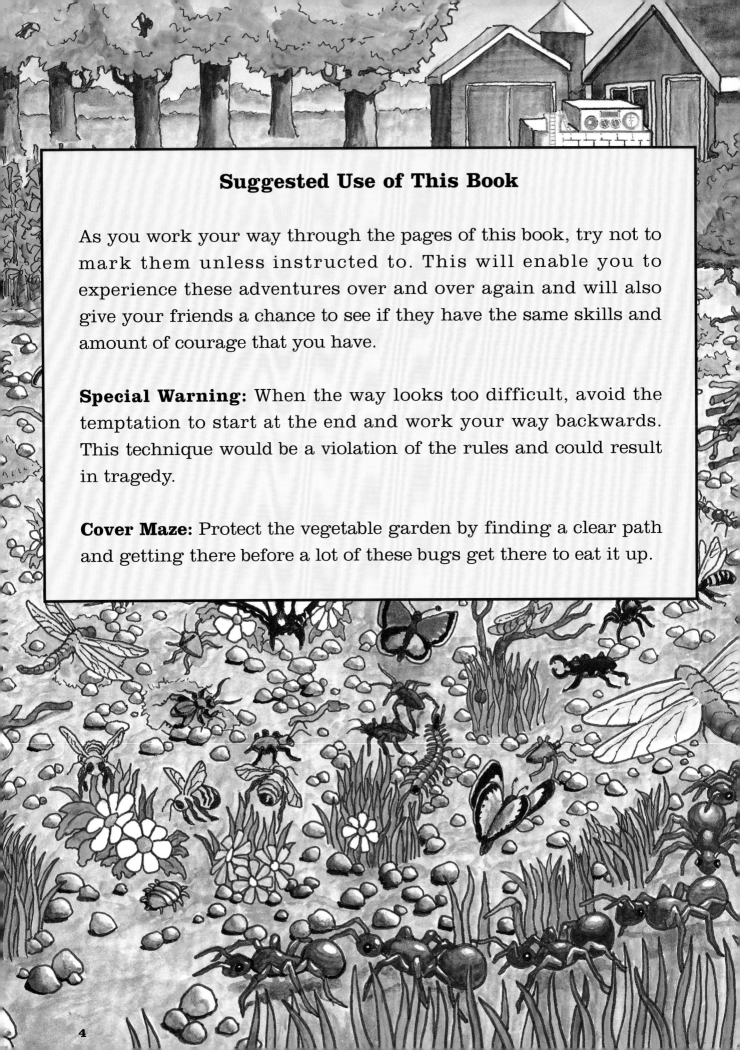

Suggested Use of This Book

As you work your way through the pages of this book, try not to mark them unless instructed to. This will enable you to experience these adventures over and over again and will also give your friends a chance to see if they have the same skills and amount of courage that you have.

Special Warning: When the way looks too difficult, avoid the temptation to start at the end and work your way backwards. This technique would be a violation of the rules and could result in tragedy.

Cover Maze: Protect the vegetable garden by finding a clear path and getting there before a lot of these bugs get there to eat it up.

Introduction

Did you know that scientists estimate that there are between two to four million species of insects in the world? They flourish from the mountaintops to the valleys—wherever there is food. Have you ever noticed the abundance of bug life right out in your own backdoor or in the nearby field? We're talking about common everyday backyard bugs. Chances are you step on many of them either by accident or intentionally and think nothing of it as you journey about. Because they are so small, they usually seem insignificant and non-threatening, and most of the time go unnoticed.

It would be quite an adventure if you could reduce yourself to the size of a bug and explore their world. If you decided to take such an adventure, it would undoubtedly be very frightening and dangerous. They could possibly see you as a threat or mistake you for a good meal. There are some, too, that are downright mean. But these facts would only heighten the adventure.

Here you have a chance to take such an adventure. Should you have the courage to journey forth, learn all you can and try to do good along the way. Observe the bugs close up and where you find them doing damage, do what you can to stop them.

This experience will not be easy. Once you start, be determined not to turn back no matter how difficult the going gets. Remember, in reality these are only little backyard bugs.

Background Information

The common backyard bugs are the ones you might see every day. You will want to get to know the ones you will encounter by their common name, so study the bug manual and be able to identify them. Many of these bugs cause damage in various ways, some are harmless, some do good, and one is very dangerous. Here is a brief summary:

Termites: Eat wood and can destroy a home if not stopped.
Snails and slugs: Will eat plants and can destroy a vegetable garden.
Aphids: Suck the juices from plant leaves and can kill the plant.
Grasshoppers: Eat plant leaves.
Tomato and corn worms: Eat vegetables.
Ants: Harvest the sugars from aphids, helping to kill plants.
Earwigs: Destroy fruits and flowers but aid farmers by eating snails and caterpillars.
Cockroaches: Dirty and spread germs on everything they touch.
Centipedes: Eat bugs.
Bees: Produce honey and pollinate vegetables and flowers.
Ladybugs: Eat aphids.
Black widow spiders: Very poisonous and dangerous.
June bugs: Eat fruit.
Tarantulas: Eat bugs.
Monarch butterflies: Destructive to crops as worms before they become butterflies.
Praying mantis: Eat ladybugs and other bugs.
Dragonflies: Eat harmful insects.

An important thing to remember is that you can't judge the bug by its look. It might not look like a destructive bug. For example, the tiny aphid can destroy an entire vegetable garden, and the beautiful tomato worm can eat up a tomato before it moves onto the next one. Termites, in quantity, can severely damage a house in time. On the other hand, the honey bee does a great deal of good for mankind and is not dangerous unless you harm it.

So, with all of this in mind, good luck, stay brave, and don't give up.

The Bug Manual

Learn the names of these common bugs. Write the number indicating the bug's name in the box to the left of the drawing of each bug.

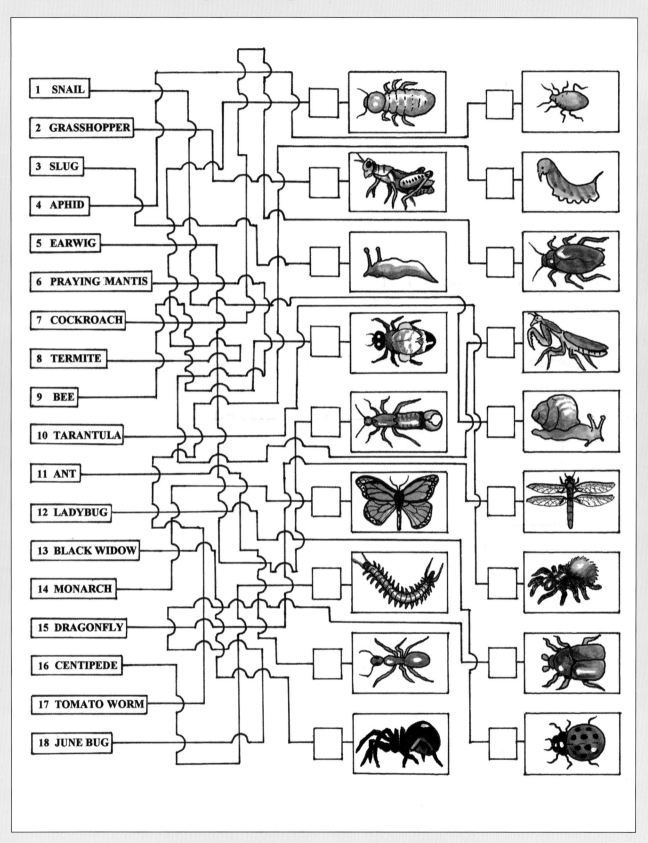

1 SNAIL

2 GRASSHOPPER

3 SLUG

4 APHID

5 EARWIG

6 PRAYING MANTIS

7 COCKROACH

8 TERMITE

9 BEE

10 TARANTULA

11 ANT

12 LADYBUG

13 BLACK WIDOW

14 MONARCH

15 DRAGONFLY

16 CENTIPEDE

17 TOMATO WORM

18 JUNE BUG

The Sizing Machine

Find the path through each level and shrink yourself to miniature size.

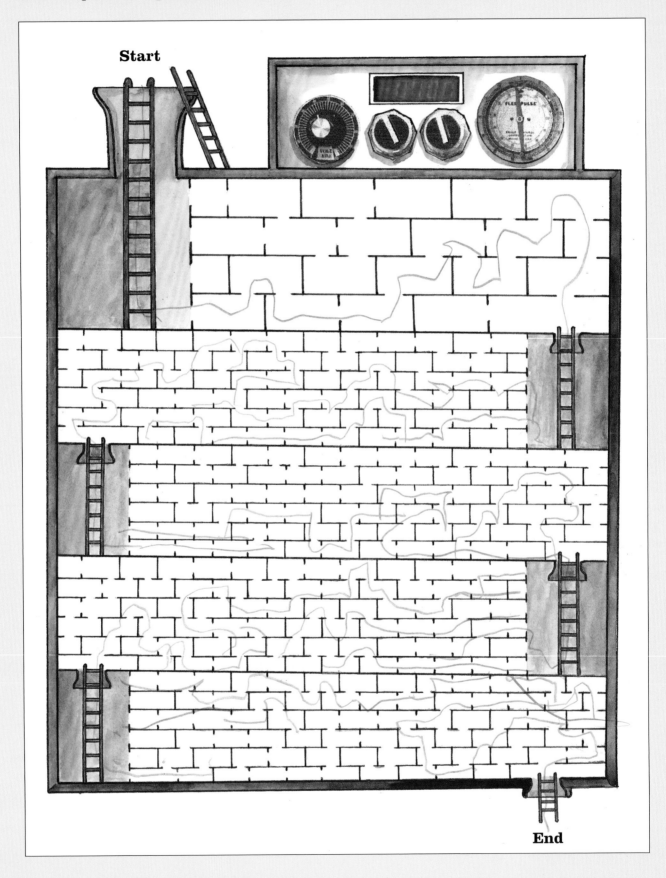

The Scrap Wood Pile

Let's see what's under that old pile of wood. Find a clear path.

Termites

Find a clear path through the eaten-out wood grooves to the group of termites on the right.

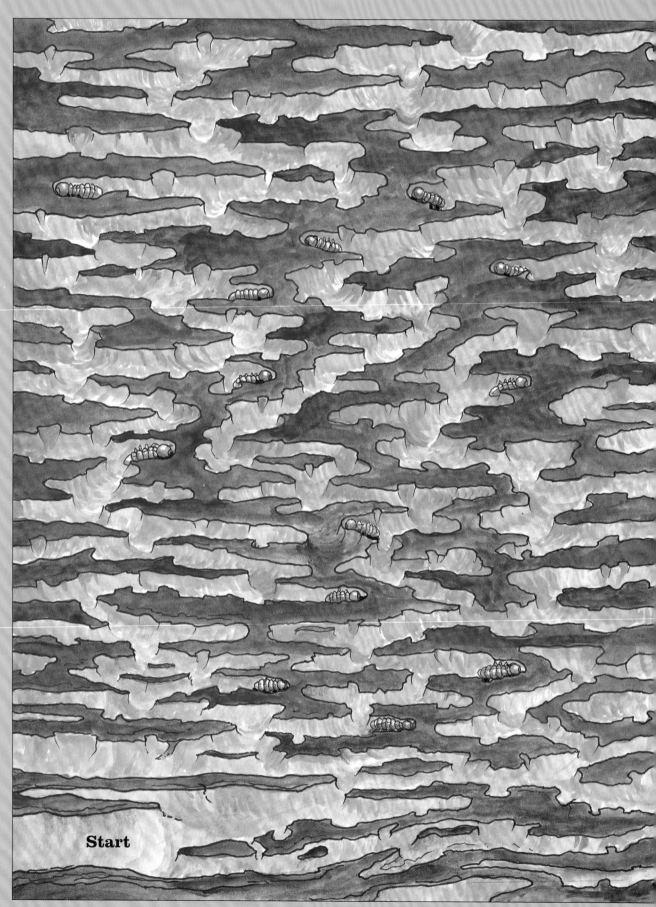

Start

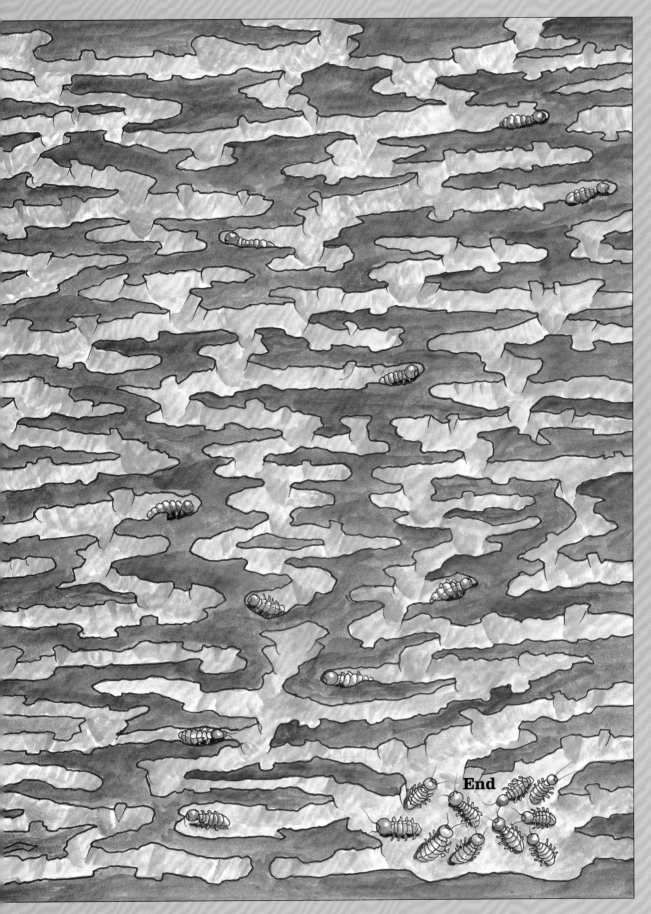

End

Earwigs

Find a clear path past the earwigs.

Start

End

13

Cockroaches

These roaches like it cool and damp. Find a clear path to the sunlight.

Start

Tarantula

This tarantula has several entrances to its den. Find out which ones.

End

Centipedes

Find your way to each centipede, then find out which one has the most legs.

Put the number in each box.

Monarch Butterfly

On the branches are three stages of development of the monarch butterfly. Find your way to the butterfly by following one branch system. You cannot pass a thorn.

Start

End

June Bugs

These June bugs have damaged many figs and are about to damage more. Avoid the damaged figs. Move on the good figs and onto all figs with a June bug to knock it off.

Start

Do not backtrack or cross over your path.

End

Praying Mantis

The praying mantis eats ladybugs. Hurry to save the ladybug. Move from flower to flower and avoid flowers with ladybugs on them.

Start

End

Dragonflies

The yellow dragonfly has a slight tear in its wing. Help it find a way to rest on the blade of grass by finding a clear path through these swarming dragonflies.

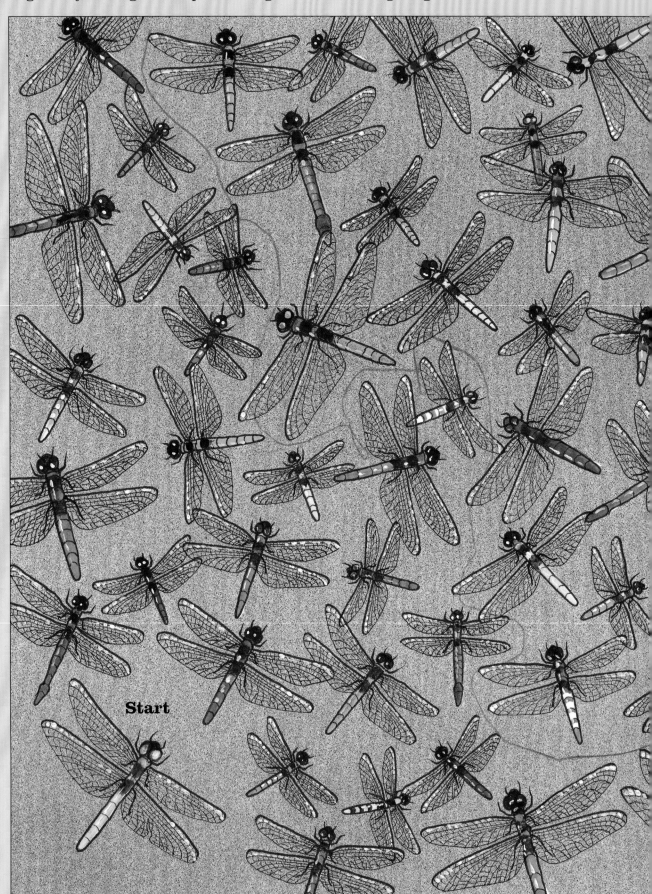

Start

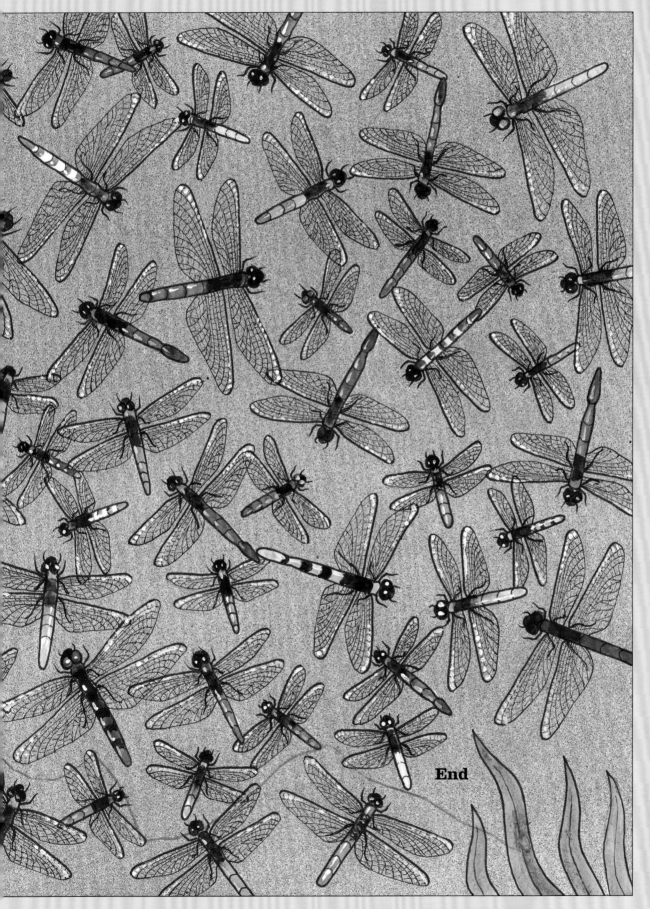

End

The Backyard

Find a clear path in this backyard to the pile of wood.

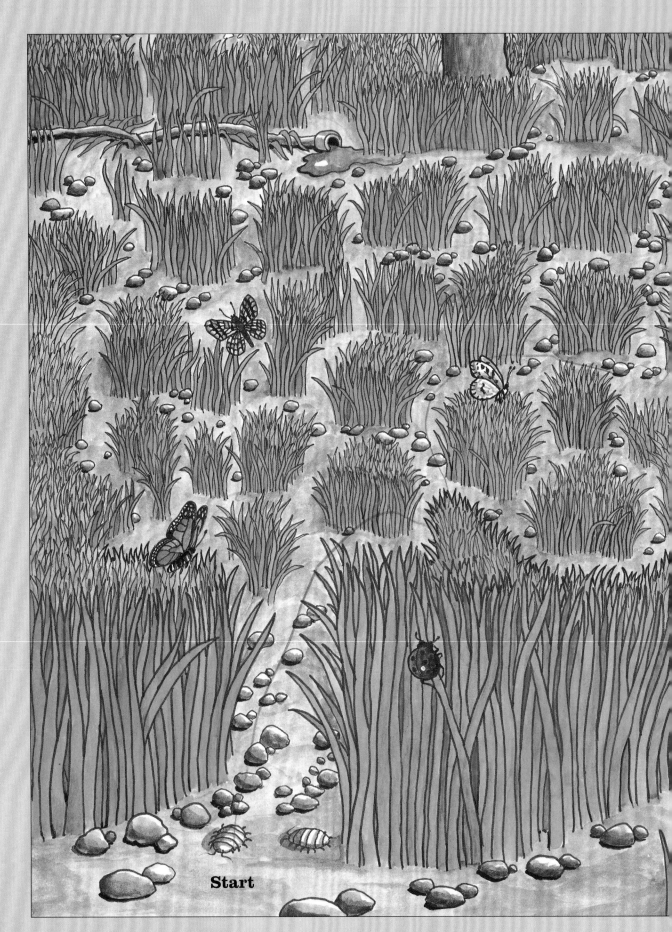

Start

End

Black Widow Spider

The black widow spider is dangerous. Have courage and find a path on its web to get a close-up look at its face. Avoid the babies.

Start

End

Ant Hole

Escape from the black widow spider by finding a clear path to the safety of the ant hole.

Start

End

Ant Colony

Travel through the ant colony by finding an unblocked path.

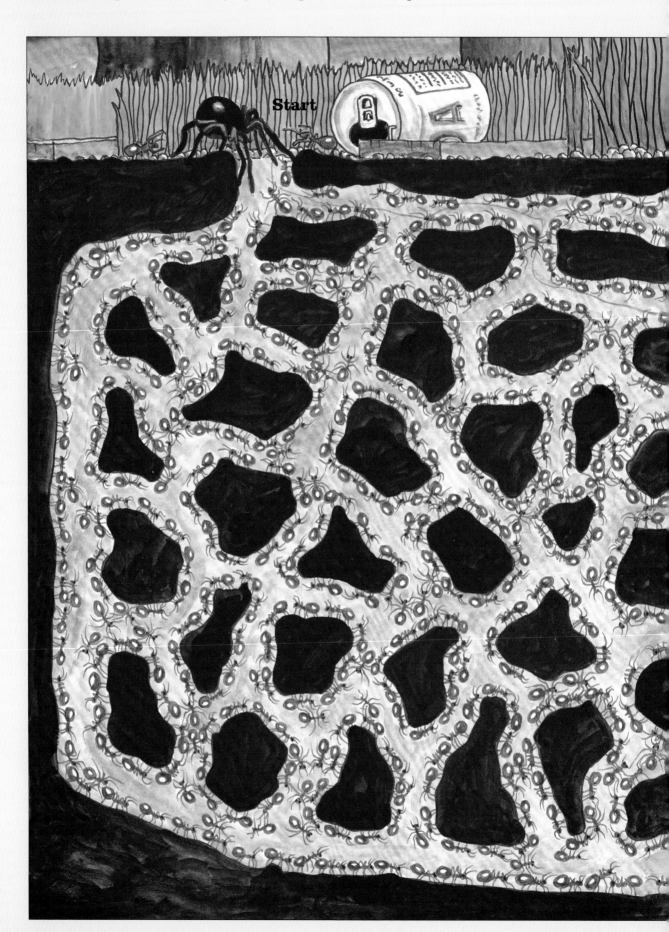

Start

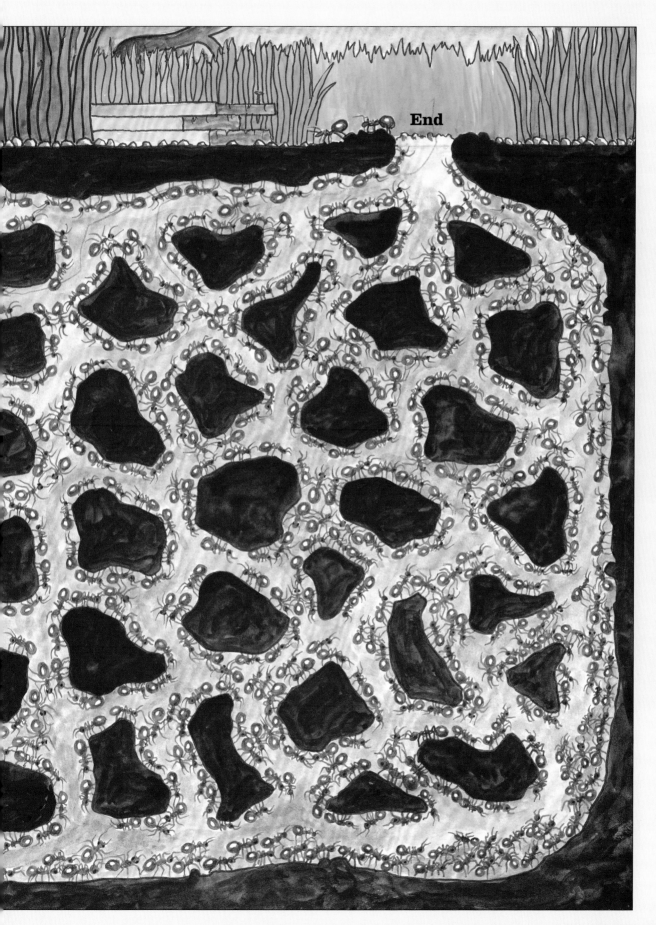

End

Attack of the Ants

The ants are heading for the vegetable garden. Find out why by finding a clear path to the garden.

Start

End

Aphids

These plants are covered with aphids, which will destroy them. Ladybugs eat aphids, so you can save the plants by placing a ladybug on each one.

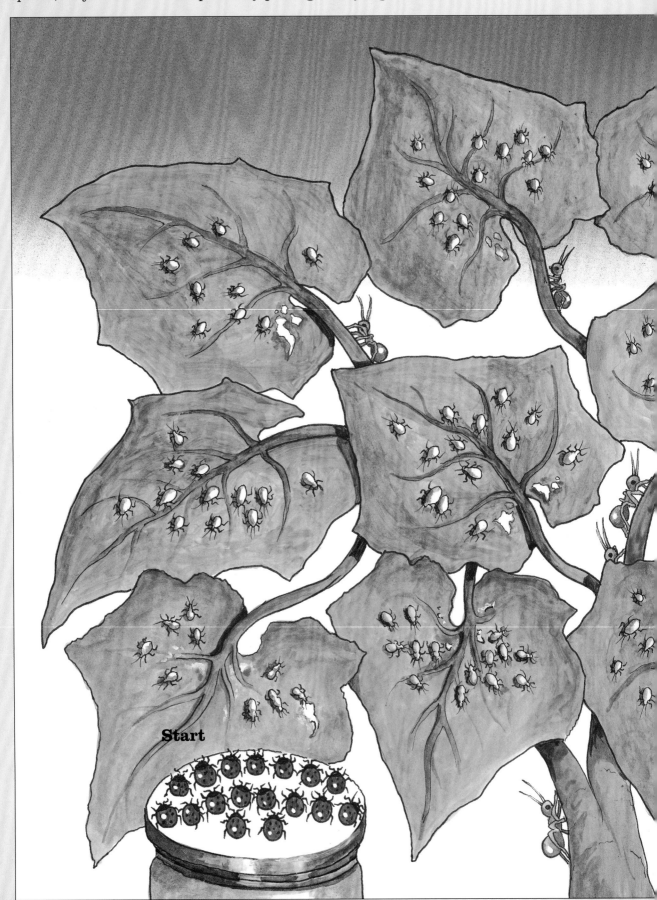

Start

Lead these ladybugs from start to finish by hopping from one leaf to the next. Touch each leaf only once. Do not backtrack or cross over your path.

End

Grasshoppers

The grasshoppers will eat these string beans if you don't stop them. Move through the string beans to knock off the grasshoppers. Stay off the white space.

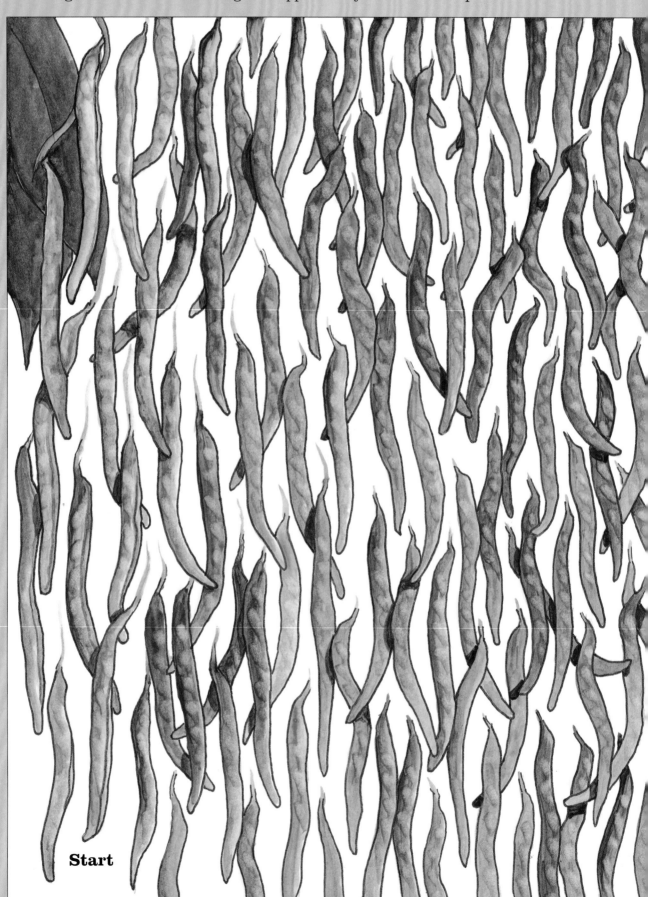

Start

End

Tomato Worms

These worms will destroy the nice tomatoes. Starting from the bottom, make your way up and around the support frame to knock off each worm. Do not backtrack or cross over your path.

More Tomato Worms

Continue on the support frame until all worms have been knocked off.

Snails and Slugs

The strawberry patch is in big danger. Find a clear path to the water valve.
Open the valve to fill the ditch with water, and you will save the strawberries.

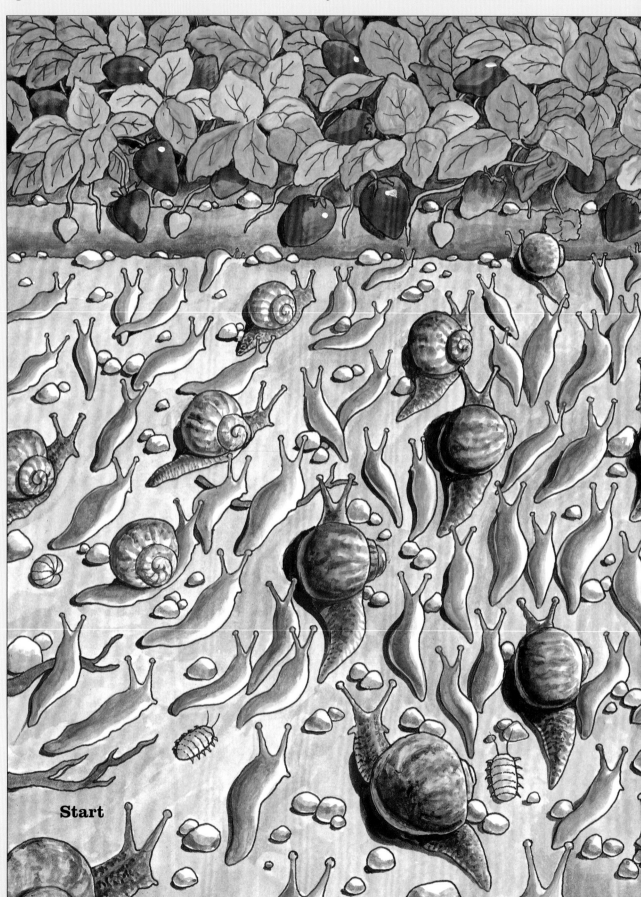

Start

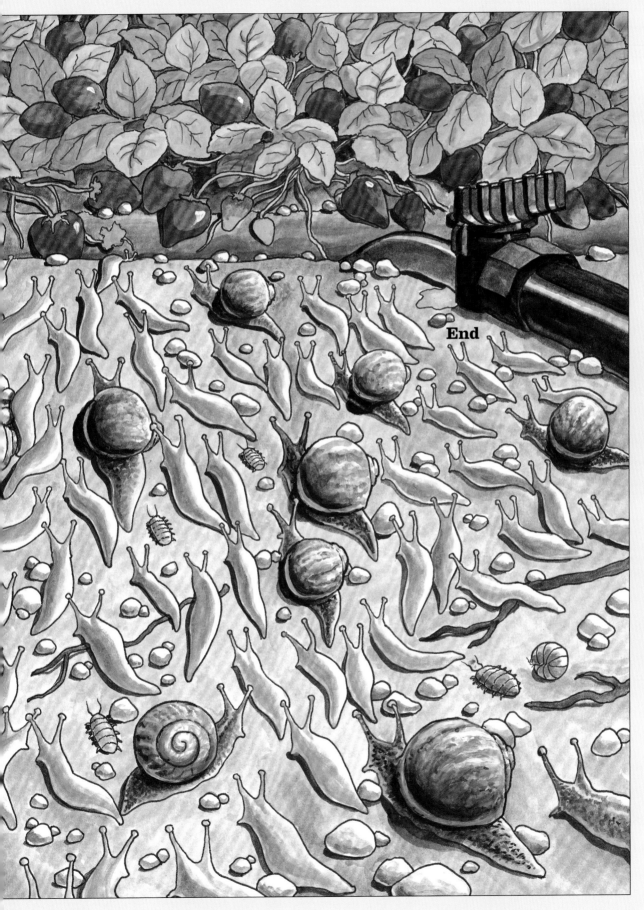

Corn Worms

These ears of corn are in danger of being eaten by the worms. You can save them by removing each worm. To do this, find a path on the kernels of corn past each worm. Don't backtrack or cross over your path. Don't cross over any gaps between the kernals of corn.

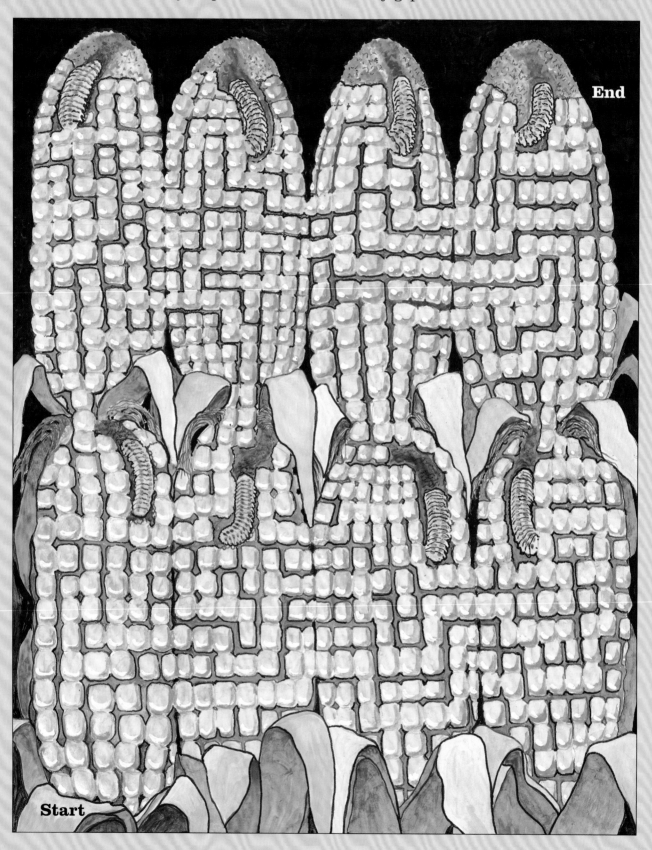

Honey Bee

Help this honey bee find its way home by finding a clear path to the hive.

Hive

Explore this hive. Move on the honey-filled cells through the hive to the exit. Avoid empty cells and bees.

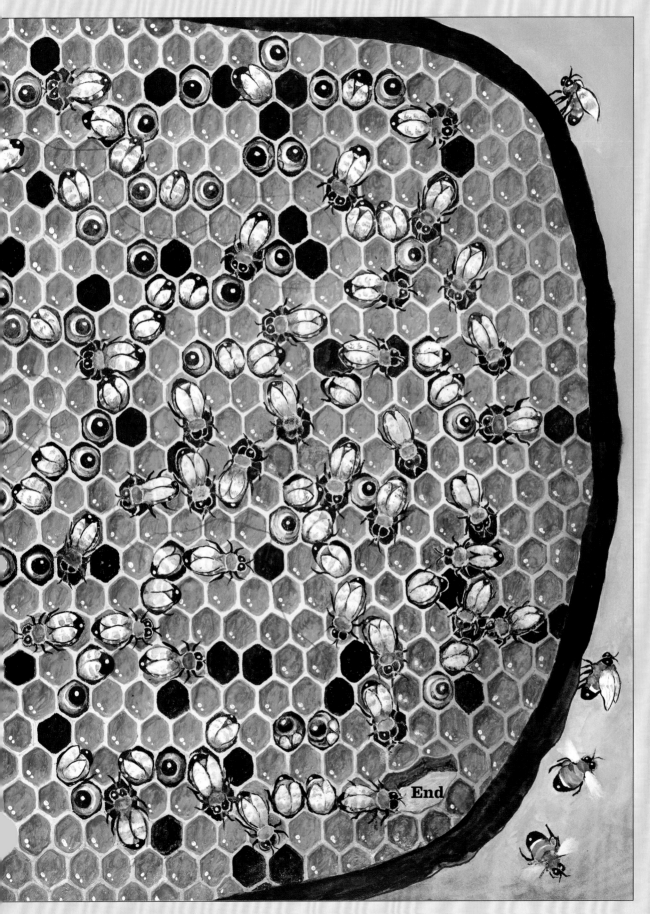

End

The End of the Day

Find a clear path to the size machine. It's time to end the day.

Start

End

Back Into the Sizing Machine

Begin at the bottom and find a path through the cells to return to normal size.

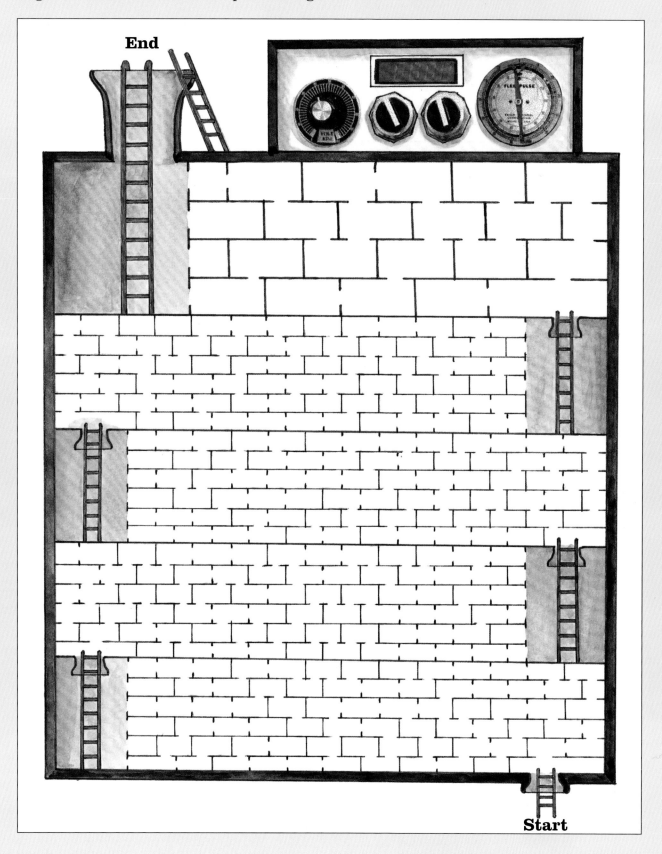

Congratulations!

You have successfully experienced a romp around the backyard with many of the common bugs you will find there. Undoubtedly, you have had to face some pretty frightening and dangerous bugs, but you did not back off or fail to complete the tasks at hand. You have gone into dark realms and explored beautiful flower patches. You've been instrumental in saving the family vegetable garden by demonstrating courage in the face of daunting odds. You've learned that right in your backyard the bug world can be an interesting and unique place and full of danger—especially if you're reduced to the size of the bugs themselves.

If you have any problems, the solutions to each maze are on the following pages.

Cover Maze

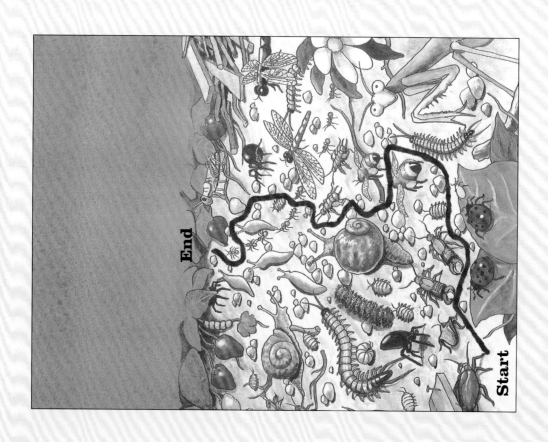

The Bug Manual

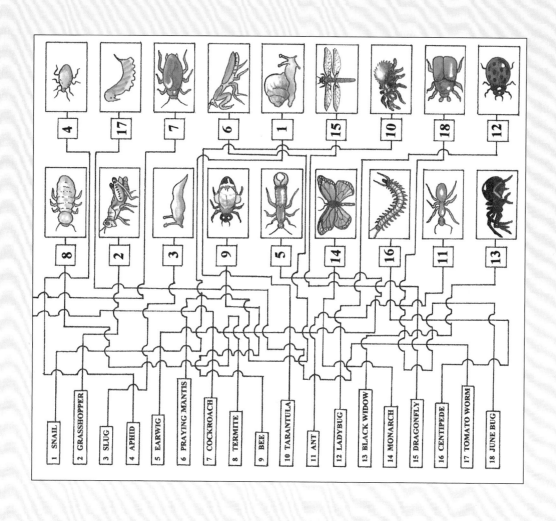

1 SNAIL
2 GRASSHOPPER
3 SLUG
4 APHID
5 EARWIG
6 PRAYING MANTIS
7 COCKROACH
8 TERMITE
9 BEE
10 TARANTULA
11 ANT
12 LADYBUG
13 BLACK WIDOW
14 MONARCH
15 DRAGONFLY
16 CENTIPEDE
17 TOMATO WORM
18 JUNE BUG

The Sizing Machine

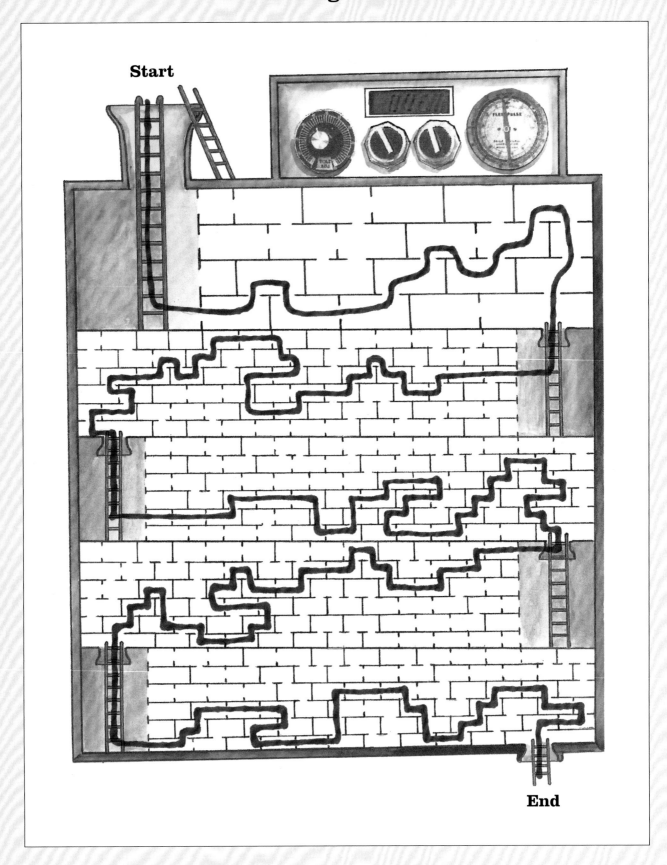

The Scrap Wood Pile

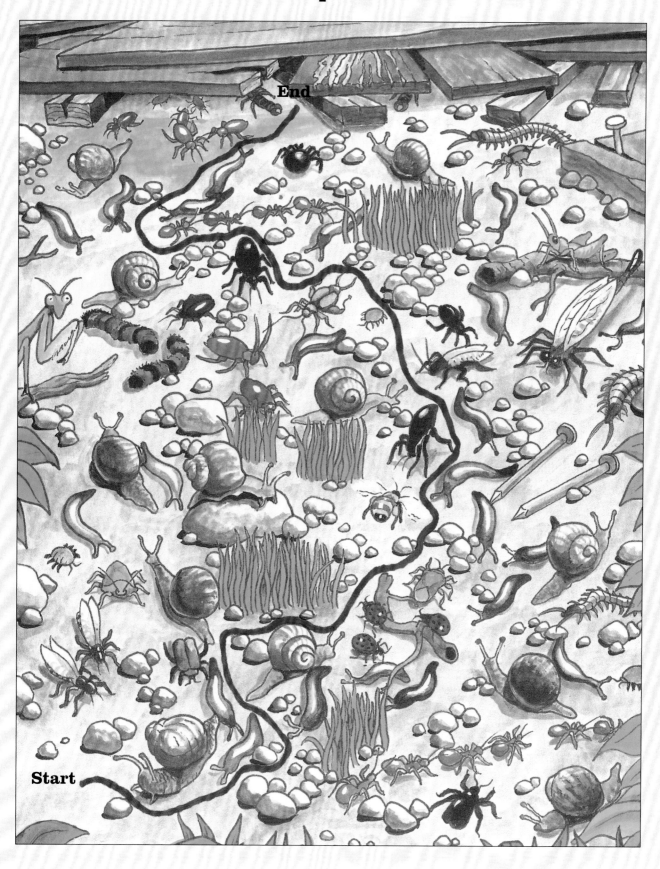

Start

End

Termites

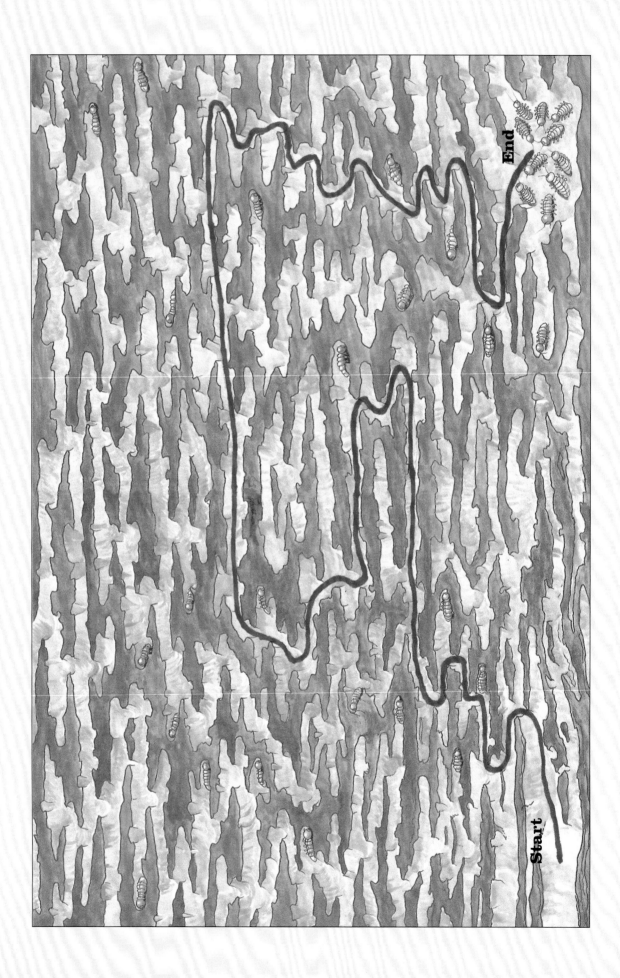

Earwigs

Start

End

Cockroaches

End

Start

Tarantula

Start

End

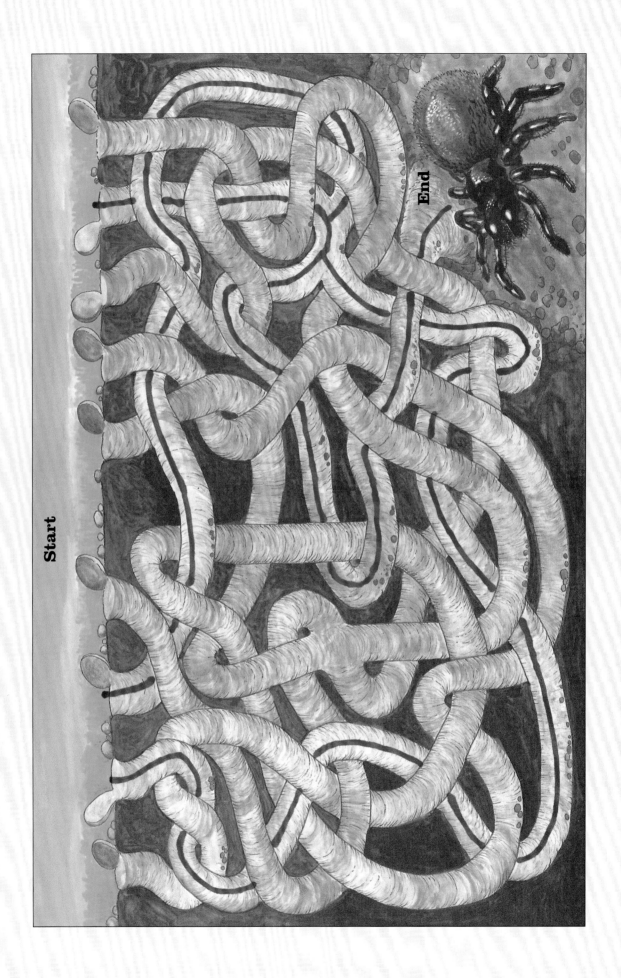

Centipedes

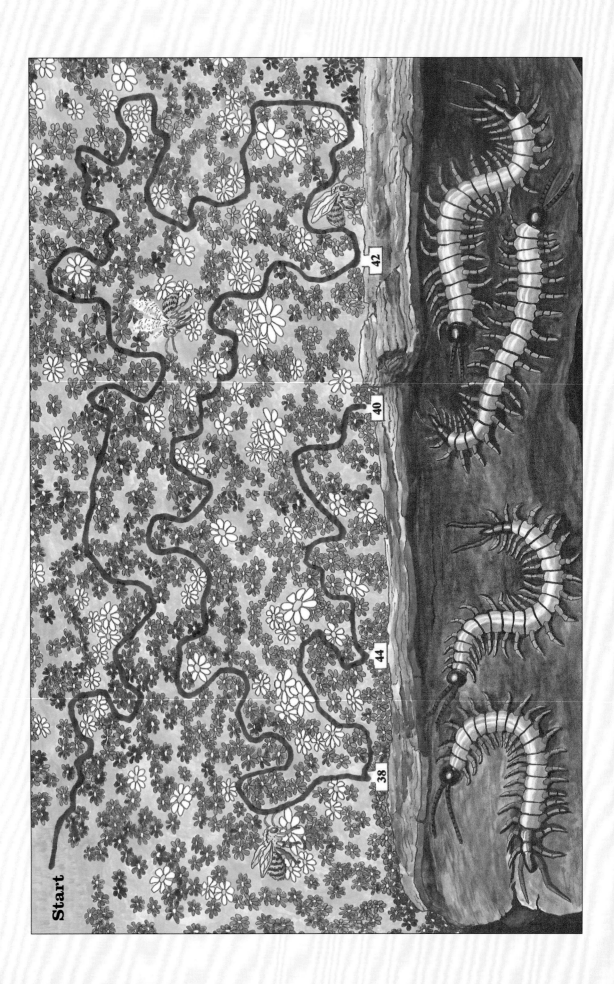

Start

38

44

40

42

Monarch Butterfly

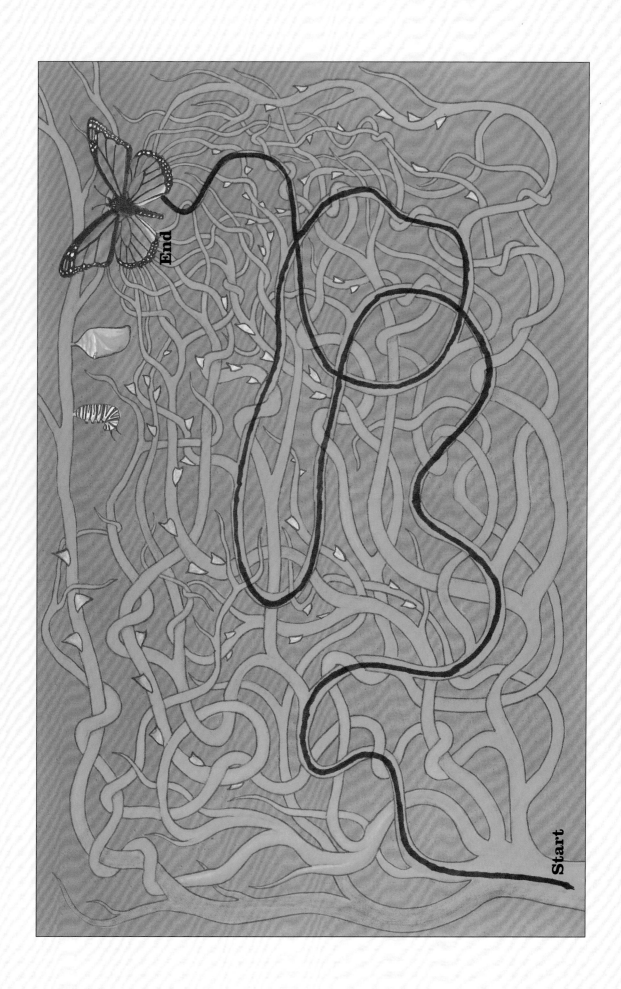

Start

End

Start

End

Praying Mantis

Dragonflies

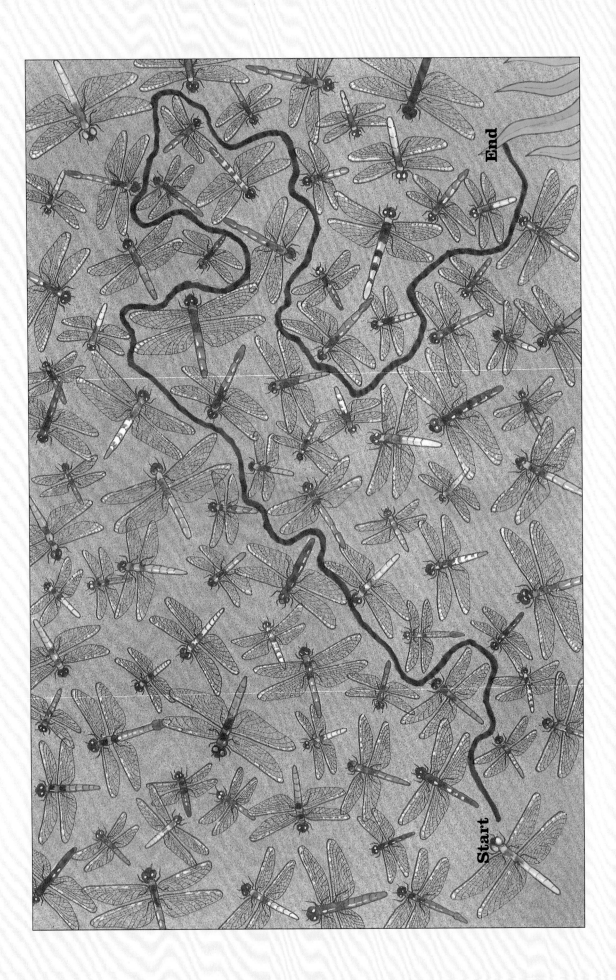

The Backyard

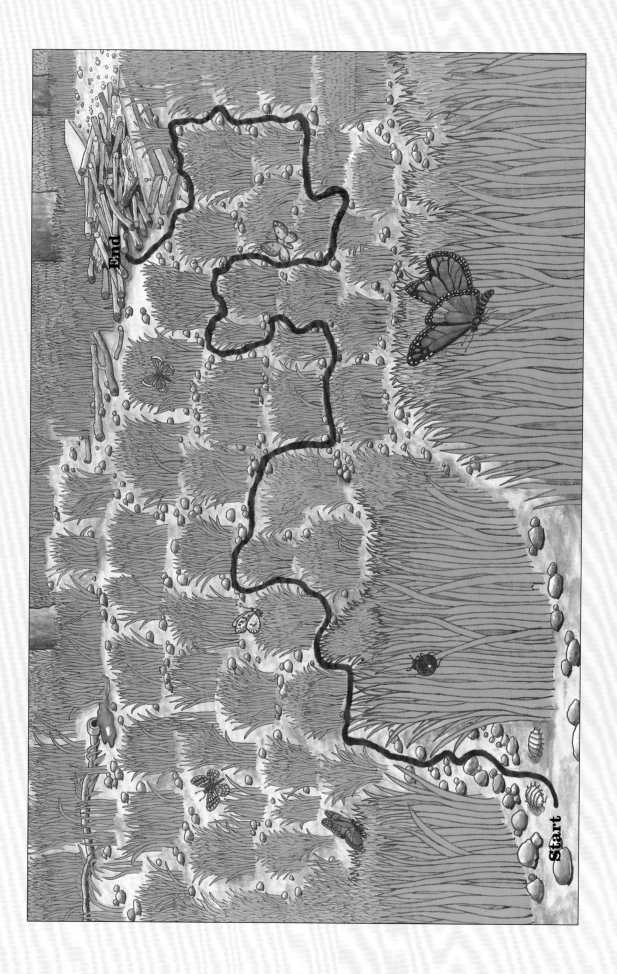

Black Widow Spider

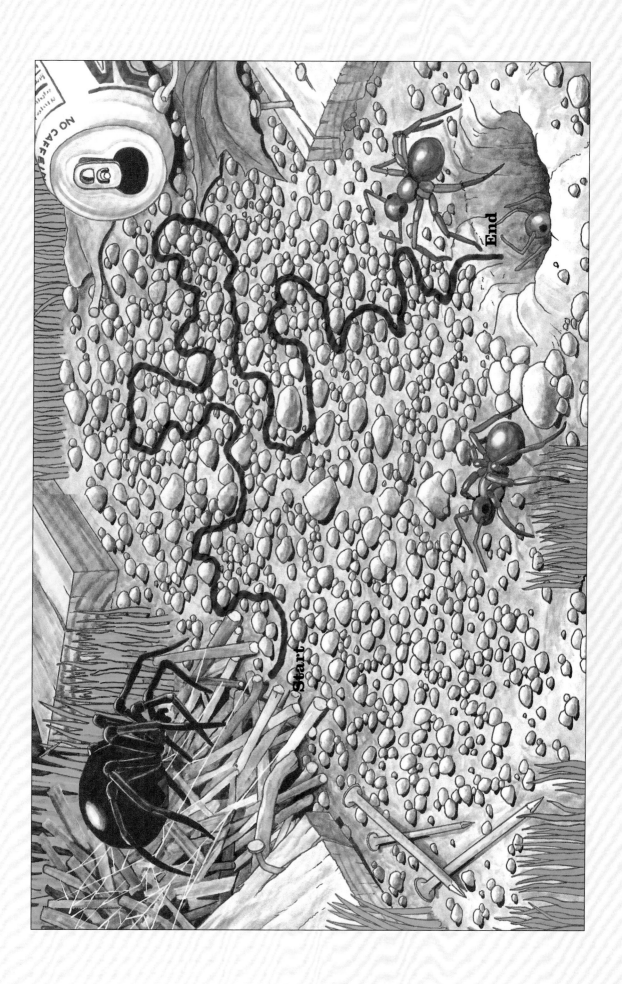

Ant Colony

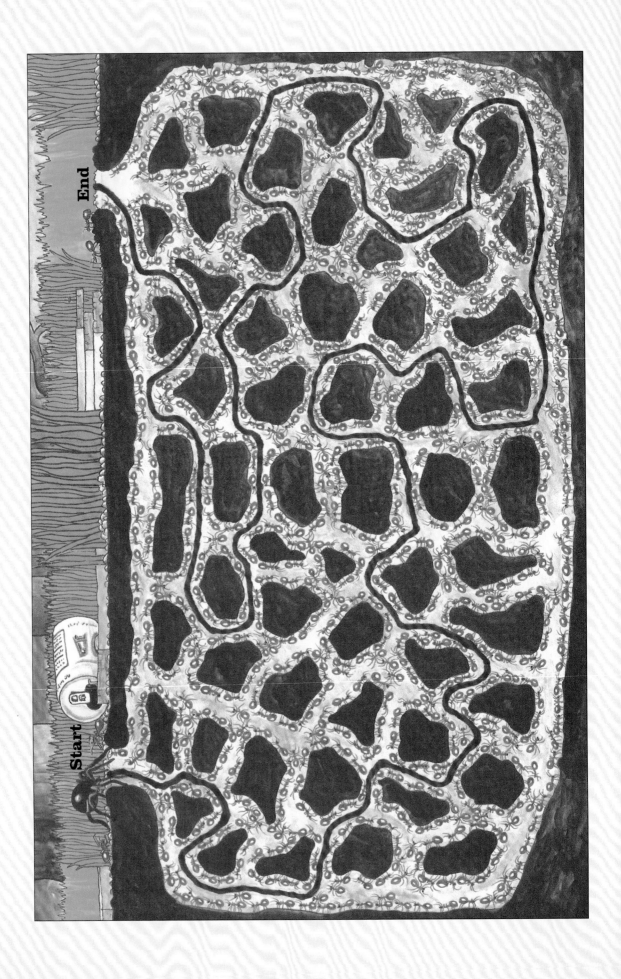

Attack of the Ants

Start

End

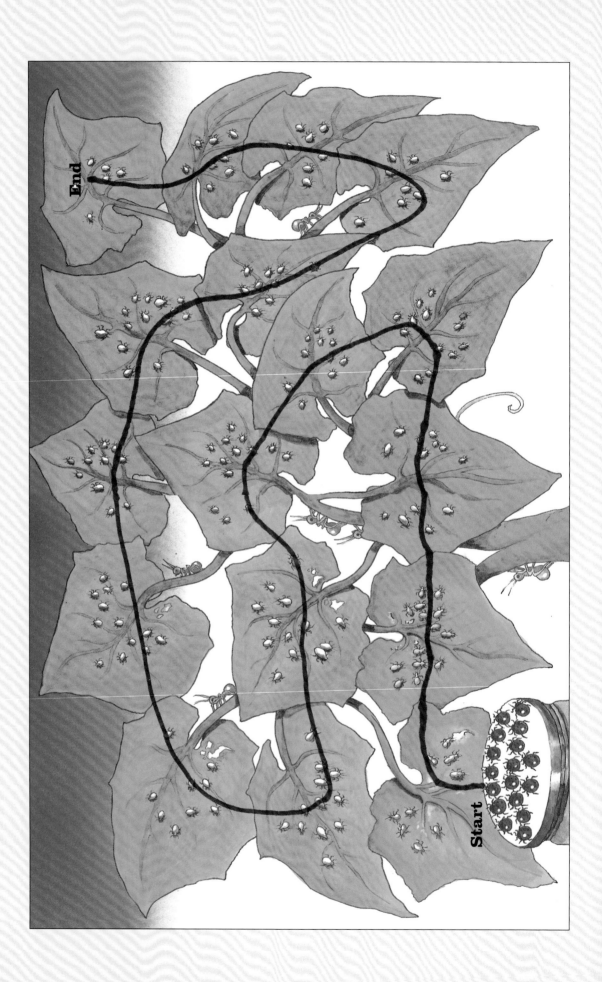

Start

End

Grasshoppers

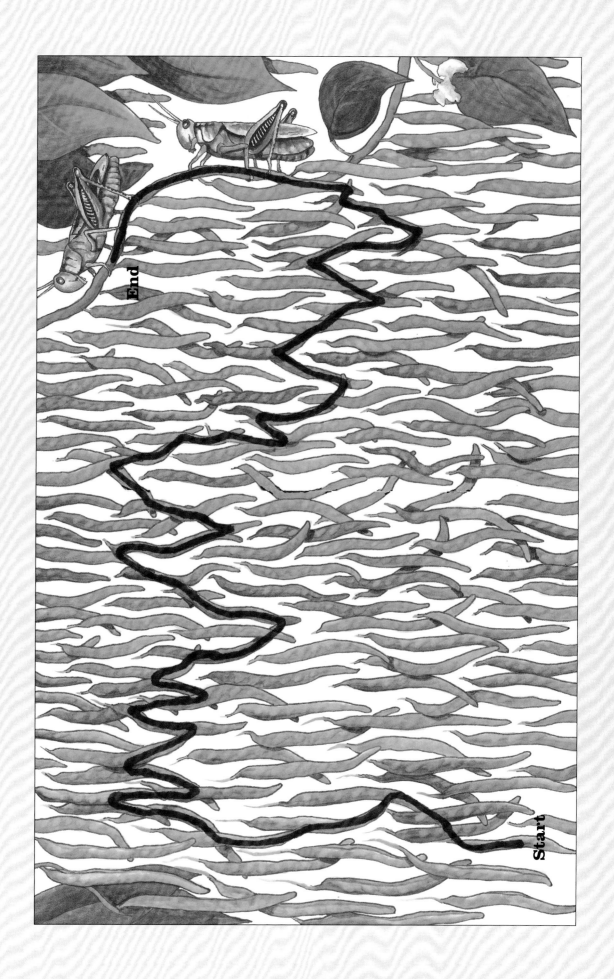

Tomato Worms

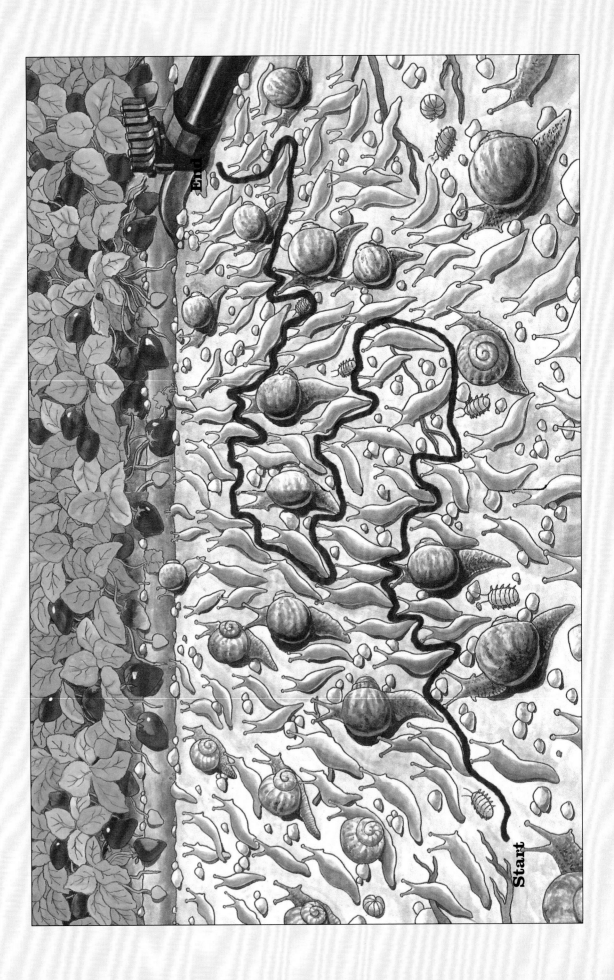

Start

End

Corn Worms

End

Start

Honey Bee

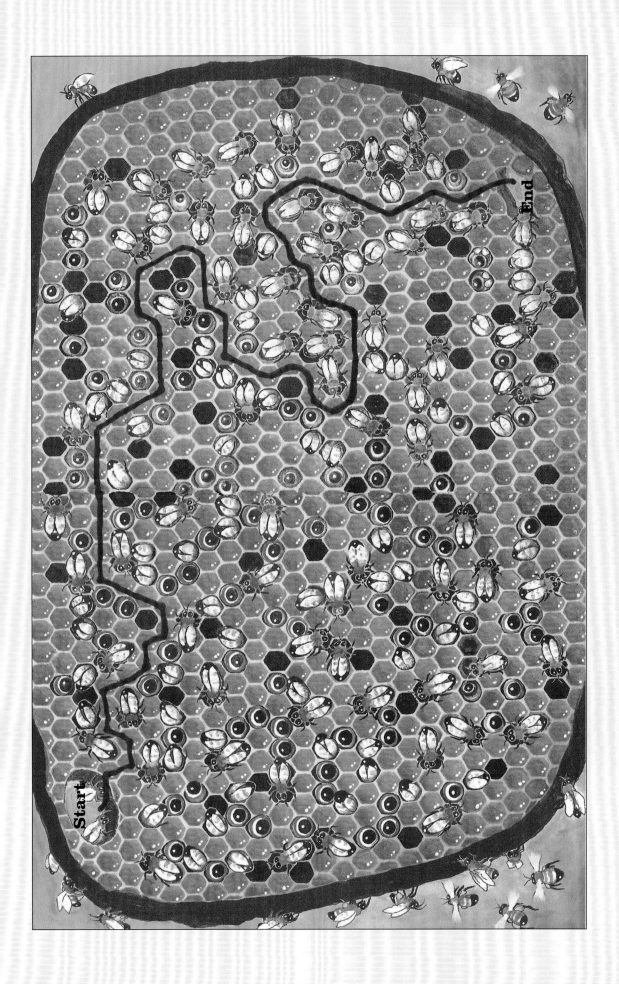

Hive

Start

End

The End of the Day

Back Into the Sizing Machine

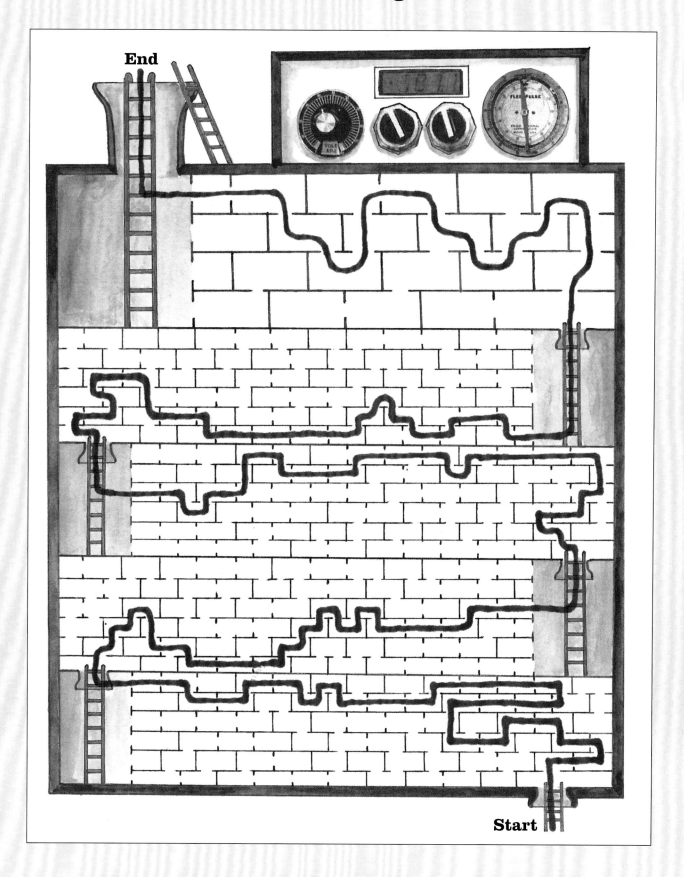

Index

Pages in **bold** refer to answers.
Ant colony, 34–35, **68**
Ant hole, 32–33, **67**
Ants, 6, 36–37, **69**
Aphids, 6, 38–39, **70**
Backyard, 28–29, **65**
Bees, 6
Black widow spiders, 6, 30–31, **66**
Bug manual, 7, **53**
Centipedes, 6, 18–19, **60**
Cockroaches, 6, 14–15, **58**
Corn worms, 6, 46–47, **75**
Dragonflies, 6, 26–27, **64**
Earwigs, 6, 12–13, **57**
End of the Day, 50, **78**
Grasshoppers, 6, 40–41, **71**
Hive, 48–49, **77**
Honey bee, 47, **76**
June bugs, 6, 22–23, **62**
Ladybugs, 6, 38–39, **70**
Monarch butterflies, 6, 20–21, **61**
Praying mantis, 6, 23–25, **63**
Scrap wood pile, 9, **55**
Sizing machine, 7, 51, **54, 79**
Snails and slugs, 6, 44–45, **74**
Tarantulas, 6, 16–17, **59**
Termites, 6, 10–11, **56**
Tomato worms, 6, 42–43, **72–73**

Books By Roger Moreau

Around the World Mystery Mazes: An A-Maze-ing Colorful Adventure!
Backyard Bug Mazes: An A-Maze-ing Colorful Adventure!
Dinosaur Escape Mazes: An A-Maze-ing Colorful Adventure
Dinosaur Mazes
Great Escape Mazes
History Mystery Mazes: An A-Maze-ing Colorful Adventure!
Lost Treasure Mazes
Mountain Mazes
Natural Disaster Mazes
Space Mazes
Treasure Hunt Mazes: An A-Maze-ing Colorful Journey!
Undersea Adventure Mazes: An A-Maze-ing Colorful Journey!
Volcano & Earthquake Mazes
Wildlife Mazes: An A-Maze-ing Colorful Journey Into the Wild!
Wild Weather Mazes
Wizard Magic Mazes: An A-Maze-ing Colorful Quest!